HANBURY HALL

Worcestershire

THE NATIONAL TRUST

Hanbury is 4½ miles east of Droitwich, 1 mile north of the B4090, 6 miles south of Bromsgrove, 1½ miles west of the B4091.

Acknowledgements

This guidebook owes much to previous editions by Michael Gibbon and Anthony Mitchell, and to James Lees-Milne's *Country Life* articles of 1968. Thanks are also due to Selby Clewer, formerly the Trust's administrator at Hanbury, and to Margaret Gent, whose dissertation on Hanbury (Birmingham Polytechnic, 1992) revealed much important new documentary evidence. The staff of Worcestershire Record Office have also been unfailingly helpful.

Jeffrey Haworth
Gervase Jackson-Stops
1994

Photographs: Conway Library, Courtauld Institute of Art pp. 42, 43; Cooper-Hewitt Museum, New York p. 19; *Country Life* pp. 9, 27, 31(above), 37 (below); *Country Life*/Julian Nieman pp. 8, 11 (above and below), 14, 25; Courtauld Institute Galleries p. 13; English Life Publications Ltd, Derby, p. 45; National Trust pp. 40, 44; NT/Erik Pelham p. 17; National Trust Photographic Library pp. 7, 18, 29, 31 (below), 36, 37 (above), 38; NTPL/Jonathan M. Gibson p. 23; NTPL/Nick Meers back cover; NTPL/Alasdair Ogilvie pp. 5, 39; NTPL/Stephen Robson p. 34; Worcestershire Record Office/Geoffrey N. Hopcraft p. 1; The Downland Partnership Ltd front cover, pp. 20, 21, 22; David Fitzer pp. 32, 33, 35.

ISBN 1–84359–054–9

Designed by James Shurmer

Phototypeset in Monotype Bembo Series 270 by SPAN Graphics Limited, Crawley, West Sussex (SG1900)

Print managed by Centurion Press Ltd (BAS) for the National Trust (Enterprises) Ltd, 36 Queen Anne's Gate, London SW1H 9AS

CONTENTS

INTRODUCTION

To avoid confusion, the house is assumed to face the main points of the compass, with the entrance front on the south (in reality south-east).

'A sweet place and a noble estate', John Hough, Bishop of Worcester, wrote in 1733. Surrounded by its old deer-park carved out of the ancient royal forest of Feckenham, Hanbury Hall epitomises the substantial squire's home of the reign of William and Mary. At first sight a sophisticated building of one date, it proves to have been a gradual rebuilding on an old site to a somewhat haphazard plan. The architectural details are a felicitous mixture of the up-to-date and the provincial. The date 1701, incised in Victorian numerals above the front door, probably repeats an earlier date-stone and records its general completion, while the main interior feature, the splendid wall-paintings on the staircase by Sir James Thornhill, are an afterthought of around 1710.

Edward Vernon, son of the rector, bought Hanbury in 1631, and his grandson Thomas Vernon was the rebuilder and embellisher of the old manor house, perhaps beginning soon after he inherited in 1679, and continuing until he was elected Whig MP for the City of Worcester in 1715. He was called to the Bar in 1679, was a bencher of the Middle Temple in 1703 and practised in the Court of Chancery for 40 years, amassing a fortune of £112,000 in fees, according to his own estimation. An inventory taken shortly before he died is unusually detailed, recording not only movable chattels room by room, but materials and colours of upholstery and curtains as well as some decorative schemes. It confirms that the corner pavilions contained 'apartments' on the upper floor, each comprising a principal bedchamber with a dressing-room or closet. However, the chief rooms, all with painted ceilings, were arranged on the ground floor to the

right-hand side of the house in a 'State Apartment': the Great Parlour (now the Drawing Room), the Lobby and Great Withdrawing Room (now amalgamated to form the Dining Room), and beyond them the Best Bedchamber and Dressing Room. Thomas Vernon's own working apartment consisted of a Long Gallery, closet and study in a separate building north-west of the house – and connected to it by a single-storey range of service rooms.

Vernon's architect was probably a local master mason, William Rudhall (c.1660–1733) of Henley-in-Arden, whose signature appears on a drawing for a more ambitious three-storey entrance front (see p.37), and who is later recorded supplying a chimney-piece for Hanbury in 1718. Its design and planning has much in common with Robert Hooke's Ragley Hall, only eight miles away, and William Talman's Thoresby in Nottinghamshire, both houses completed in the 1680s. It was therefore relatively old-fashioned for its date, due either to Thomas Vernon's particular preference or to the master mason's own conservatism. Formal gardens were laid out about the same time by George London, and are recorded in a detailed perspective view by the surveyor Joseph Dougharty, dated 1731–2.

Thomas Vernon's widow, Mary Keck, continued to live at Hanbury till her death in 1733, when the house was inherited by a cousin, Bowater Vernon. In 1734 he commissioned Wootton to paint his portrait (now in the Smoking Room), showing the house and garden in the background. But he died only a year later in 1735. His son, Thomas, who came of age in 1745, must have started to 'naturalise' the garden soon after that date, extending it to the south-west, and building the Orangery.

In 1771 Thomas Vernon died, leaving Hanbury to his only daughter Emma, who in 1776 married

The entrance front

Henry Cecil, later 1st Marquess of Exeter. The Cecils swept away the remains of the old formal gardens, employing the architect Anthony Keck to remodel some of the interiors (notably the Drawing Room and Library) in the latest Neo-classical taste. However, the marriage came to grief after Emma's elopement with the curate, William Sneyd, in 1789, and in the following year the contents of the house were sold at auction.

Eventually, Emma and her third husband, John Phillips, moved back into Hanbury in 1804, refurnishing the main rooms. Few structural alterations have been made since that date, apart from the creation of the present Dining Room (formerly two rooms) about 1830, and the addition of a new forecourt and pavilions designed by the antiquary and topographer R. W. Billings in the 1850s. Large-scale domestic offices were also added at the back of the house, but demolished after the Second World War.

Sir George Vernon left Hanbury to the National Trust on his death in 1940, but it was only in 1953 that the Trust was able to take on the house, thanks to an endowment provided by an anonymous donor. The family pictures and some furniture have returned, largely through the generosity of Sir George's adopted daughter and her husband, the late Mr and Mrs Frederick Horton of Shrawley Wood House. Mr R. S. Watney gave the flower pictures and porcelain collection.

Unusually amongst National Trust properties, the primary purpose of showing Hanbury Hall to visitors is combined with its use for day conferences, meetings and large dinner parties, in order to raise money for the upkeep of the property.

PLAN OF THE HOUSE IN 1721

Current room layout in brackets

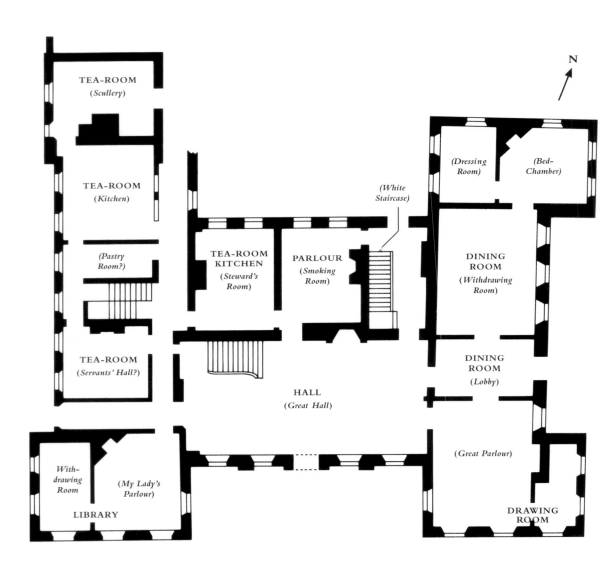

N

TEA-ROOM
(Scullery)

TEA-ROOM
(Kitchen)

(Dressing Room)

(Bed-Chamber)

(White Staircase)

(Pastry Room?)

TEA-ROOM KITCHEN
(Steward's Room)

PARLOUR
(Smoking Room)

DINING ROOM
(Withdrawing Room)

TEA-ROOM
(Servants' Hall?)

DINING ROOM
(Lobby)

HALL
(Great Hall)

With-drawing Room

(My Lady's Parlour)

(Great Parlour)

LIBRARY

DRAWING ROOM

CHAPTER ONE

TOUR OF THE HOUSE

THE HALL

The entrance to the Hall is by way of a porch, already shown in a watercolour of 1833, but glazed later in the century. People wore warmer clothes in the eighteenth century; hence the front door was originally unprotected from the elements.

The Hall occupies the whole five-bay centre of the south front and is unusual in that it incorporates the great staircase at one end of it, decorated with Thornhill's famous murals. This asymmetrical arrangement is similar to that at Fetcham Park, Surrey, built by William Talman in 1705–10, where Laguerre decorated the staircase and hall.

The late eighteenth-century floorboards probably replace stone or marble paving: the 1720/1 inventory describes 'a great Turkey workt Carpet for the floor'. The rest of the furniture included an oval table, two sideboards, a dozen black leather chairs, a gilt leather screen, and 'four Salmon Colour Cushions for the windows'. All this suggests that the Great Hall was used for dining on great occasions, though the adjoining Great Parlour would have been used more regularly when there were smaller numbers at table.

By 1790, the room was used for quite different

The Hall and Painted Staircase, before 1900

The Hall and Painted Staircase

purposes. The sale catalogue of that year describes an 'elegant mahogany billiard table' along with card-tables, backgammon and cribbage boards, a 'Mississippi table' (evidently for a gambling game invented in America), a travelling boot-jack, an engraving of the yards at Newmarket, five music stands, and a combined barometer, thermometer and hygrometer – an interesting commentary on the then owner of the house, Henry Cecil, whose wife, Emma Vernon, had just deserted him.

The finely carved panelling gives the room an architectural character, with five great arched door-cases leading to different parts of the house, and echoing the niche above the chimney-piece. The two most important arches, on the east wall, are framed by fluted Corinthian half-columns: that on the left led via a paved lobby to an external door on the east front, probably used as the everyday entrance to the house; while that on the right led into the Great Parlour. The similar arch to the right of the chimney-piece gave access to the White Staircase, and the family's bedchambers in the east range; while the one opposite the front door led to Thomas Vernon's 'Smoking Room' or study. The fifth and last arched doorcase, under the stairs, led into another paved lobby with a door to the garden at the end of it. The door to the left of this arch, leading to the present Library, is a late eighteenth-century addition: access to the room was previously from the garden lobby.

The panelling is all of pine and was evidently grained originally. Bills survive from a painter named Thomas Boulter, dated 1718, and include the Great Hall, but these unfortunately do not mention the colours chosen. However, a stony slate-blue found under many later layers may represent his work, perhaps intended to complement the background colour of the ceiling – now faded to a dull green. This change in the colour of the ceiling (and Thornhill's murals on the staircase) must have encouraged later generations to re-grain the walls, giving the room a warmer feeling. Several later layers of graining survive, including one of the 1850s, and one of about 1900, and when the room was redecorated by the National Trust in 1990 this scheme was again adopted in order to give tonal balance to the room. The character of the walnut graining is, however, more in the early eighteenth-century taste, recalling the hall at Stoke Edith in Herefordshire, the seat of Thomas Vernon's friend and contemporary Thomas Foley, where Thornhill painted the walls above grained panelling

CEILING

The 1720/1 inventory describes the ceiling as 'painted stone colour', which indicates the present monochrome scheme, with its *trompe-l'oeil* saucer domes and gardening trophies, was probably not yet in place. Indeed, Thomas Boulter's painting of the walls in 1718 may have prompted the ceiling to be freshly decorated. It does not attain the vigour of Thornhill's decoration on the Staircase, executed about 1710. Affinities with the ecclesiastical trophies and coffering of the apse of St. Alfege's, Greenwich, which appear to have been painted, at least in part, by Richard Scott in collaboration with Thornhill, suggests that the latter may have delegated this later task to him or some other assistant.

The trophies in the corners of the ceiling represent the four seasons, and include agricultural tools and musical instruments; a hunting horn and a backgammon board represent winter. It was lightly

restored over the winter of 2000/1 by the Perry Lithgow Partnership.

CHIMNEY-PIECE

The black marble bolection-moulded chimney-piece is the original, but to prevent the fire smoking, the opening was made smaller in the nineteenth century by inserting the alabaster slab which bears the Vernon motto *Vernon semper viret* ('Vernon always flourishes'). If 'Vernon' is separated into the Latin words *ver* and *non*, then it can be translated, 'the spring is not always green'.

SCULPTURE

Attributed to EDWARD STANTON (1681–1734)
Thomas Vernon (1654–1721)
The builder of Hanbury, in a wig and lawyer's

Thomas Vernon (1654–1721); attributed to Edward Stanton (Hall)

bands. Stanton, with his partner, Christopher Hors-naile, signs the monument to Thomas Vernon in Hanbury church (see p.42).

The carved oak cartouches with painted coats of arms over the doors illustrate successive Vernon marriages.

PICTURES

FLANKING CHIMNEYPIECE:

JOHN VANDERBANK (1694–1739)
Bowater Vernon (1638–1735) and his wife, Jane
These are presumably the pictures for which Bowater paid Vanderbank £52 10s on 26 August 1734. Bowater Vernon's second wife, Jane, daughter and co-heiress of Thomas Cornwallis of Aber-marlais, Carmarthenshire, was mother of his three children, including Thomas, his heir, born in 1724. The enriched frames are the originals.

Manner of MICHAEL DAHL (?1659–1743)
Captain Thomas Vernon (1686–1734) and his wife, Rachel
The younger brother of Bowater Vernon, with his wife, Rachel Jeffreys.

SOUTH WALL:

JOHN VANDERBANK (1694?–1739)
? *Phoebe Bowater, Mrs William Vernon of Caldwell*
Signed and dated 1729
Bowater Vernon's mother painted after she was widowed in 1708.

Manner of Sir PETER LELY (1618–80)
? *Jane Carter, Mrs Richard Vernon of Astwood*
The mother of the builder of Hanbury.

FURNITURE

Pieces of furniture, porcelain and other decorative items listed below with a V were at Hanbury in the nineteenth century, and have been returned to the house recently.

Pair of early nineteenth-century black lacquer chests on stands, Cantonese.

Early nineteenth-century satinwood centre-table (V).

Two small Dutch floral marquetry chests-of-drawers flanking the front door, bought for Hanbury in the nineteenth century as having a suitably William and Mary character (V).

The seat furniture includes a near pair of William and Mary chairs, a settee of about 1770, a George I cabriole-leg wing chair, and a set of four early nineteenth-century mahogany side-chairs.

Chamber organ by Samuel Green, *c.*1770. This was made for Tusmore House, near Banbury, Oxfordshire, and is so shaped because it was once combined with a harpsichord (placed on top) to form a claviorganum, one of the rarest of English keyboard instruments.

PORCELAIN

Two large mid-eighteenth-century blue-and-white Chinese Export jars with lids, and two more containing artificial flowers, on mid-nineteenth-century giltwood candlestands (V).

METALWORK

The large early-nineteenth-century hall lantern is seen in Victorian photographs of the room.

THE DRAWING ROOM

This occupies the site of Thomas Vernon's Great Parlour, which was two-thirds the size of the present room, and had an inner closet in the far corner. The 1720/1 inventory describes 'the ceiling painted by S.r James Thornhill', whose sketch for it still survives (see p.13). It was 'wainscoted with oak' and had crimson mohair curtains, and a set of ten gilt chairs, covered with crimson and white flowered velvet. As befitted a room used for dining, a large sideboard table stood against the wall opposite the chimney-piece, and a 'very large peer glass' between the two south-facing windows would have helped reflect the candlelight at night.

In the 1770s Emma Vernon and her husband, Henry Cecil, enlarged the parlour by amalgamating it with the closet and pushing the east-facing window further out so as to square the room up. Their architect was almost certainly Anthony Keck of Worcester, for the plasterwork frieze with its restrained Neo-classical urns and anthemions, and the green and white marble chimney-piece, can be paralleled at other houses where he was employed.

(Above) The Drawing Room

(Right) Detail of the painted decoration on the satinwood pier-table, c.1780, in the Drawing Room

DECORATION

At some later stage after 1790 the walls appear to have been hung with green silk, to judge by a few threads discovered during the recent restoration work. This may well have been done in 1829, after Emma's third husband, John Phillips, moved out of Hanbury, passing the house on to her distant cousin Thomas Tayler Vernon. Vernon and his wife, Jessie Foley, could also have commissioned the rare stencilled border painted on the floorboards. This survived intact on the north side of the room, and has recently been extended by the National Trust round the other three sides.

The present green flock wallpaper is a copy of an eighteenth-century pattern found in a house in St Stephen's Green, Dublin. A flock paper of similar scale and colour, with a pattern of tiny birds, was subsequently discovered to have been in this room at one stage.

Having lost its original furniture many years ago, the room is now used for dinner parties, meetings and lectures.

PICTURES

GEORGE WEBSTER (fl.1797–1832)
A Frigate and other vessels in a Squall
Panel
From the Vernon collection, formerly at Shrawley Wood.

Sir HENRY WEIGALL (?1800–83)
Harry Foley Vernon (1834–1920) and Thomas Bowater Vernon (1832–59) as children, 1836

Sir HENRY WEIGALL (?1800–83)
Auda Letitia Vernon, Mrs T. A. Hill (1862–1957)
Daughter of Sir Harry Vernon.

MELCHIOR DE HONDECOETER (1636–95)
Peacocks and Farmyard Fowl
On loan from the Polesden Lacey collection, Surrey.

FURNITURE

Gilt pier-table (V), *c.*1780, with a satinwood top, painted with floral garlands and grisailles. This could be one of the pieces bought back by the family at the 1790 sale.

Rosewood break-front bookcase (V), listed in the library in an inventory of 1829. It contains the remnants of the Vernon family's library, returned in 1991.

Pair of Regency mirrors, the friezes incorporating coloured plates from D'Hancarville's four-volume catalogue of Sir William Hamilton's collection of antiquities, published in Naples between 1766 and 1776.

Late eighteenth-century-style chimney-glass from Brockhampton by Bromyard, in Herefordshire.

Piano by Broadwood, *c.*1817. In full working order, it was bequeathed to the National Trust by John Gillespie Pattison in 1982. It is a duplicate of the famous instrument supplied to Beethoven.

METALWORK

ON TABLE BY DOOR:

A remarkable covered monteith in lacquered and gilt tin, probably early eighteenth-century.

THE DINING ROOM

This was formerly two rooms: described as the Lobby and the Withdrawing Room in the 1720/1 inventory. Both had painted ceilings by Thornhill, which still survive, clearly showing the position of the original partition wall. The window facing the door to the Hall was then an exterior doorway leading to a walled forecourt, probably used as the everyday entrance to the house by Thomas Vernon and his family, while the front door was reserved for important visitors. In the Lobby the panelling, or wainscot, was 'painted with Stars', according to the inventory, while in the Withdrawing Room it was 'painted walnuttree' (ie grained to resemble walnut). Beyond this room lay the Best Bedchamber and Dressing Room, both with painted ceilings, completing Thomas Vernon's 'state apartment'. Around 1780, these were transformed into a library, but this was in turn lost when a fireproof staircase was inserted in the north-east 'pavilion' in the 1860s.

The proposal to amalgamate the Lobby and Withdrawing Room is first seen in a drawing of 1830, signed by the Yorkshire-born architect Matthew Habershon, who worked at two other houses near Droitwich: Mere Hall, which he altered

and extended *c*.1826, and Hadzor House, which he rebuilt in 1827. It is not known how many of his proposals for Hanbury were adopted, but Thomas and Jessie Vernon, who married in 1831 and began to raise a family soon afterwards, must have needed a larger dining-room, and almost certainly made the change before 1837, the year of Thomas's premature death.

DECORATION

The six plasterwork panels surrounding the original Withdrawing Room ceiling are likely to be contemporary with Thornhill's painting, and feature garlands of oak and laurel, and acanthus scrolls in the two smaller rectangles. The other four panels, surrounding the lobby ceiling, are rather less boldly modelled and were evidently made to match when the partition wall was removed and the ceiling repositioned about 1830.

The dado rail and skirting were introduced at the same time as the yellow flock paper in the 1960s.

James Thornhill's sketch for his ceiling paintings in the Great Parlour (now Drawing Room), Lobby (called Vestibule), and Withdrawing Room (now Dining Room) (Witt Collection, Courtauld Institute Galleries)

FIREPLACE

The position of the fireplace was also changed about 1830, but the elaborately carved Rococo chimney-piece and overmantel date from about 1760, and could have been commissioned by Thomas Vernon, the builder's grandson, about the same time as he built the Orangery. The carving, in softwood, part grained and part gilded, is reminiscent of the engraved designs of the London carver Thomas Johnson, but is probably the work of a talented local using features from Johnson's pattern books, like the mythical ho-ho birds (derived from Chinese lacquer and porcelain patterns) which perch precariously on the broken pediment. The bolection-moulded chimney surround and the hearth are evidently earlier, and could be the 'Chimney peice & slab of Coloured marble' listed in the Withdrawing Room in 1720/1.

The Dining Room

CEILING PAINTINGS

The smaller of the two ceilings, once in the Lobby, is in a restricted palette of browns and blues (apparently much restored) and shows Boreas, the North Wind, abducting the nymph Oreithyia, the daughter of a legendary King of Athens. The subject would have been particularly appropriate for a draughty passage room with an external door facing north-east.

Thornhill's ceiling painting in the state bedchamber beyond this room (destroyed in the nineteenth century) depicted Endymion, who was cast into a profound sleep by Zeus, in return for eternal youth, with Selene, the goddess of the moon, and Morpheus, the god of sleep.

The larger painting here, which is in full colour, and was once over the Withdrawing Room, apparently depicts Apollo, the Sun God, parting from Clymene, the mother of Phaeton, to conduct the chariot of the sun across the heavens - an appropriate subject for a room in receipt of morning light. The hound left behind may refer to his time as the herdsman of King Admetus. Thornhill's sketch for the two ceilings is now in the Witt collection at the Courtauld Institute, London (see p.13).

PICTURES

NORTH WALL:

JOHN VANDERBANK (1694?–1739)
Thomas Vernon, MP (1654–1721)
Shown wearing his lawyer's bands.

Sir GODFREY KNELLER (1646/9–1723)
Mary Vernon (d.1733)
She married Thomas Vernon in 1680.

WEST WALL BELOW:

Sir JOSHUA REYNOLDS, PRA (1723–92)
Emma Vernon (1755–1818)
The only child and heir of Thomas Vernon II, she was married by her ambitious mother to Henry Cecil, later 10th Earl and 1st Marquess of Exeter, in 1776. The marriage was a disaster and in 1789 she eloped with the local curate, William Sneyd; they were married two years later after her divorce from Cecil. Perhaps cut down from a larger picture.

SOUTH WALL:

ENGLISH, nineteenth-century
Thomas Vernon (1832–59) and *Sir Harry Vernon* (1834–1920)
Sons of Thomas Tayler Vernon and Jessie Foley, and successive owners of Hanbury.

EAST WALL:

Hon. JOHN COLLIER (1850–1934)
Doris, Lady Vernon (d.1962)
The last member of the Vernon family to live at Hanbury.

FURNITURE

Mahogany dining-table and set of 26 chairs, in the manner of Gillows of Lancaster, c.1835.
Mahogany sideboard with inlaid panels of rosewood, c.1800.
Serving table, c.1820.

PORCELAIN

Part of a large Chamberlain Worcester service with the Vernon crest and motto, c.1830s.

TEXTILES

The carpet was specially woven in Turkey in 1992–3.

THE PARLOUR

Originally known as the Smoking Room, this was evidently Thomas Vernon's own study and office at the very centre of the house, with windows overlooking the comings and goings in the service courtyard to the north, and with the steward's room immediately adjoining to the west. In Vernon's day it contained 'two pairs of Racks to hold guns w.th 5 fowling peices & 2 bullet guns thereon'. There was a picture of Gustavus Adolphus, King of Sweden (the Protestant hero much beloved by the Whig squirearchy) above the pier-glass; a 'scriptore' or writing desk; a barometer; eight green and gold leather chairs; and 'a great Chair of stuff damask red and green', which matched the curtains and window seats.

Known later in its history as the Oak Room, presumably when the panelling was grained, it remained very much a male preserve. Both the panelling and the bolection-moulded marble chimney-piece are original. Paint scrapes on the back of the door revealed four layers of paintwork with brown, white and stone colour in descending order below the graining.

PICTURES

JOHN WOOTTON (1682–1764)

Bowater Vernon (1683–1735) *with Hanbury Hall and its formal garden*
Vernon paid Wootton £108 18s on 9 September 1734, almost certainly for this picture. He had moved into the house the previous year, on the death of Thomas Vernon's widow, Mary, but was to enjoy the property for barely two years before his own premature death. The layout of the formal garden seen in the background agrees in almost every respect with the bird's-eye view made by Joseph Dougharty in 1732 (see p.29). The gilt-gesso frame is original.

ENGLISH, eighteenth-century
Pair of portraits of children, reputedly a brother and sister of the Alcock family
Formerly hung at Cattespoole, near Tardebigge.

ERNEST STUVENS (1657–1712)
Summer Flowers
From the Watney collection.
Series of engravings of late seventeenth-century court beauties.

CERAMICS

The English porcelain was given by Mr Watney. (Handlists are available.) The Chinese Export porcelain c.1730 above the fireplace was probably ordered by Bowater Vernon.

TEXTILES

The carpet is a Heriz from northern Iran.

THE LIBRARY

Leading out of the Hall, by the left-hand door beneath the stairs.

At the time of the 1720/1 inventory, there were two rooms here, occupying the ground floor of the south-west pavilion: 'my Ladys parlour' and a smaller closet beyond which was her 'withdrawing room next the parlour'. The former was hung with no fewer than 102 pictures (probably small engravings), and its contents included a sideboard, ten chairs with blue and white flowered velvet covers, a black (presumably ebonised) pier-glass and candle-stands, blue and white curtains trimmed with scarlet fringe, and scarlet and white striped window seats. The little withdrawing-room beyond had an Oriental theme, with 'Nine India pictures in black frames', 'a Japan Corner Cupboard' and 'Japaned tea table'. It was doubtless used by Mrs Vernon and her most favoured guests as a place to indulge the fashionable (and at that time very expensive) pastime of taking tea. An external door led from here directly into the garden, giving a vista down a long *allée* to the bowling green.

After their marriage in 1776, Emma Vernon and her husband, Henry Cecil, amalgamated the two rooms, and, as in the Drawing Room, the crisply carved chimney-piece and delicate Neo-classical frieze and ceiling can be attributed to the architect Anthony Keck. It is difficult to identify the room with absolute certainty in the 1790 sale catalogue, but it was probably the 'Dining Parlour', containing 'blue queens damask festoon window curtains', eighteen mahogany dining-chairs and a set of dining-tables.

The windows on the west wall were enlarged in the 1830s, and have recently been altered so as to give access to the garden. The room is now furnished as a library, and was painted blue by the National Trust in the 1970s.

PICTURES

The engravings were given by Miss Christie-Miller.

FURNITURE

Mid-Georgian mahogany breakfront bookcase, from the Lloyd-Johnes bequest, which houses some of the later Vernon family papers.

The pair of Regency bookcases and the ceramics displayed in them are from the Watney collection (see separate handlist).

The pair of smaller bookcases between the windows is probably Edwardian.

Regency ormolu chandelier, originally intended to burn colza oil.

THE PAINTED STAIRCASE

The stairs rise from the west end of the Hall in three flights with oak balusters, carved, turned and fluted with great skill by Thomas Vernon's joiner. The parquetry on the landings is also of exceptional quality. The marks on the inside walls show that there was originally a wooden dado here, echoing the balustrade. This was removed about 1710 to make way for the painted rustication and grisaille and gold plinths supporting Thornhill's great scenes.

MURALS

At the end of the seventeenth century a painted staircase was an important status symbol for a rich man. Thomas Vernon determined to have a painted staircase at Hanbury and secured the services of James Thornhill, later to become famous for his work in St Paul's Cathedral.

Sir James Thornhill (1675–1734) belongs to the trio of master-decorators who carried all before them between the restoration of King Charles in 1660 and the death of Queen Anne in 1714. The other two are Antonio Verrio and Louis Laguerre. The style of painting they employed was inaugurated in England by Verrio, who was a native of Lecce in southern Italy, but had worked under

Bowater Vernon (1683–1735) with Hanbury Hall and its formal garden; by John Wootton, 1734 (Smoking Room)

Charles Le Brun at the court of Louis XIV. An exceedingly lively painter, he decorated vast areas of wall-space, for the King and others, in the exuberant manner of Le Brun. His approach was to paint the room or staircase to represent an open-sided pavilion without a roof. Scenes at ground level were shown between columns on the walls, while in the sky – that is to say on the ceiling – gods and goddesses were painted flying or reclining on clouds.

Laguerre and Thornhill were contemporaries and younger than Verrio. Both continued the Verrio manner and both were extensively employed. Thornhill, however, who was of an independent, not to say aggressive, temperament, elbowed his rival out of the important commission for the cupola of St Paul's. In this manoeuvre he was aided

by the fact that he was an Englishman and a Protestant, whereas Laguerre was a Frenchman and a Catholic. These considerations had weight with the trustees of St Paul's. Thomas Vernon, as a patriotic Whig, perhaps had the same ideas.

Thornhill was, towards the end of Queen Anne's reign, at the height of his career. He had already painted the Sabine Room at Chatsworth in Derbyshire (1706–7) and was engaged on his masterpiece, the Painted Hall at Greenwich Hospital (1708–12). But the work that probably impelled Vernon to commission him was the hall and staircase at Stoke Edith Park, finished by him in 1705 for Thomas Foley. Thornhill also worked next door to Hanbury at Hewell Grange for the 2nd Earl of Plymouth.

The ceiling of the staircase shows an assembly of the classical deities. The figure of Mercury breaks across the painted cornice, his head in the ceiling, his heels on the wall. With his upraised hand he points to a portrait of the notorious Dr Sacheverell (a print, flying in the air and about to be set fire to by the torches of the Furies). This is a political allusion and dates the ceiling to 1710, or soon afterwards. It is not included in Thornhill's preliminary drawing for the ceiling and south wall in the Cooper-Hewitt Museum, New York.

In 1709 the Whig party formed Queen Anne's government. They were vigorously prosecuting the war against Louis XIV with the Duke of Marlborough as commander-in-chief. The Tories were lukewarm for the war and regarded by the Whigs as little better than traitors. On Guy Fawkes Day 1709, a High Church clergyman, Dr Henry Sacheverell, preached a sermon of Tory bias in St Paul's Cathedral. The Whigs maintained the sermon was contrary to the constitutional principles of the

Revolution Settlement of 1688 and therefore seditious. Sacheverell was impeached, found guilty of sedition and forbidden to preach for three years. But the country was seen to sympathise with him. The populace of London demonstrated in his favour, and even the Queen, it was said, was on his side. Sacheverell, personally, was an unctuous hypocrite, but his trial, which took place in February 1710, made him a popular martyr. Thereafter the Queen gradually dismissed her Whig ministers and replaced them with Tories, who made peace with France at the Treaty of Utrecht in 1713.

The trial of Dr Sacheverell was a political blunder on the part of the Whigs. It was said that 'they decided to roast a parson, but made the fire so high they scorched themselves'. Thomas Vernon, as a strong Whig, no doubt regarded Sacheverell as the

The carved oak balusters and tread ends at the foot of the Painted Staircase

*Thornhill's drawing for the staircase
ceiling and west wall (Cooper-
Hewitt Museum, New York)*

(Left) An Assembly of the Gods, with Hermes (bottom) holding a print of Dr Sacheverell: the ceiling of the Painted Staircase

(Right) Achilles choosing the spear: the west wall of the Painted Staircase

blackest of traitors, fit only to be roasted and burnt to ashes by the torches of the Furies.

Thornhill's signature, *'J Thornhill pinxit'*, appears on a scroll carried by the boy directly below the figure of Hermes. At the four corners of the ceiling are cartouches with the monogram of Mary Keck and Thomas Vernon. The walls of the staircase illustrate the classical story of the life of Achilles as it appears in Homer's *Iliad* and Ovid's *Metamorphoses*.

The paintings were restored by Michael Gibbon in 1954–5. The ceiling has been lightly re-restored by the Perry Lithgow Partnership over the winter of 2001/2, and the walls will follow.

CEILING:

An Assembly of the Gods
Zeus with his eagle, Aphrodite attended by a winged Eros, Dionysus raising a cup, and Athene in armour and plumed helmet can all be recognised. Below, Chronos or Father Time with his scythe puts the Furies to flight, and Hermes, as the messenger of the gods descends from Mount Olympus to the human world below the cornice.

MAIN WEST WALL OPPOSITE LANDING:

Achilles choosing the spear
It had been foretold that if Achilles went to the Trojan war, he would not return alive. His mother, the goddess Thetis, persuaded him to dress as a girl and hide himself among the daughters of King Lycomedes. Ulysses disguised himself as a pedlar

and, taking a pack of jewellery amongst which he had placed some soldiers' arms, made his way to the court of Lycomedes. While the girls at court seized on the jewels, Achilles, still in female dress, picked up a spear and shield. Thus Ulysses found him out and carried him off to the war.

BELOW (MONOCHROME):

Agamemnon removes Briseis, Achilles' concubine
Achilles sulks in his tent.

NORTH WALL, OPPOSITE WINDOWS:

Thetis and Hephaestus
Thetis, Achilles' mother, went to Hephaestus to ask for a suit of invulnerable armour for her son. Hephaestus, with his one-eyed smiths, the Cyclopes, is seen at work, while Thetis watches from a cloud.

The armour was, however, unavailing. Achilles was killed by an arrow which struck him in the heel, the one part of his body Thetis had not dipped in the River Styx, in another attempt to make him immortal.

BELOW (MONOCHROME):

Achilles and Chiron
Achilles as a boy was instructed in a variety of arts by Chiron, the wise centaur.

ON LANDING:

Ajax and Ulysses contending for the armour of the dead Achilles
A council of Greek commanders finally awarded the armour to Ulysses, whereupon Ajax went mad and killed himself.

ON WINDOW WALL:

Military trophies

MONOCHROME PAINTINGS BELOW WINDOWS:

(These do not form part of the story of Achilles)

RIGHT:

Pan, Apollo and Midas
Pan and Apollo held a musical contest. All agreed that Apollo's polished performance on the lyre was far superior to Pan's rustic whistling. The one exception was King Midas, who said he preferred Pan's music, whereupon Apollo, not a good loser, transformed King Midas's ears to those of an ass.

LEFT:

Apollo and Daphne
Eros, out of spite, shot an arrow into Apollo, which made him fall in love with the first nymph he saw. He saw Daphne, whereupon Eros shot another arrow, which made her wish at all costs to preserve her virginity. A long chase ensued, until Daphne in despair prayed to Zeus for assistance. Zeus kindly turned her into a laurel tree *(daphne* in Greek), thus foiling Apollo, who thenceforth wore and awarded crowns of its leaves.

THE BLUE BEDROOM

The 1720/1 inventory calls this room 'the Chamber over the great hall, painted wth. Cedar & perl colour mouldings'. At that date it contained a four-post chintz bed, lined with 'sky coloured Sarsnet' or sarcenet (a thin silk material), and there were chintz-covered chairs and sarcenet window curtains to match.

At a later stage, perhaps in the 1750s, the room was painted a stony white, the basis for the present colour scheme, found under later layers of blue. In the 1790 sale catalogue it was the 'Blue Room', but still contained the original bed with its 'Chintz furniture lined with blue silk'.

(Left) Thetis and Hephaestus: the north wall of the Painted Staircase

(Right) The early eighteenth-century angel bed from Zeals House, Wiltshire (Blue Bedroom)

PICTURES

The seventeenth- and eighteenth-century Dutch and Flemish flower paintings are from Mr Watney's collection, also the fine Jean-Baptiste Monnoyer (1634–99) above the chimney-piece.

FURNITURE AND TEXTILES

The angel bed comes from Zeals House, the Wiltshire home of the Chafyn-Grove and Troyte-Bullock families, where it had always been until acquired by the National Trust in 1977 with a generous grant from the Merrill Trust. It can hardly have been the bed in which Charles II slept at Zeals, as tradition would have it, because its original hangings date from about 1730-5. They have retained their strength and colour through being preserved from light and being made of worsted (or woollen) damask. The damask design is traditional in style, the form of the pineapple dating from 1725,

that of the leaves from the 1730s. It is an appropriate acquisition for Hanbury, where a number of beds furnished with fine fabrics were disposed of in the 1790 sale.

The quilt on the bed was worked by Judith Newman, who was born in 1764 as the eldest daughter of Thomas Newman of Worcester, one of a large family of talented and prosperous Quakers living in Worcester, Leominster and Hereford in Georgian and Victorian times. Edward Newman, naturalist and author, was her nephew. As she never married, the quilt passed through her youngest sister Maria, wife of John Bradley of Worcester, and their granddaughter Caroline, wife of William Henry Ellis of Anstey Grange, Leicestershire, to their great-grandson Roger Ellis, who gave it to Hanbury in 1978.

Parcel-gilt pier-glass with the Vernon coat of arms carved in the pediment, possibly commissioned by Thomas Vernon II. It is difficult to identify in the 1790 sale catalogue, but may be one of the pieces bought in by the family.

A pair of early eighteenth-century Dutch marquetry chairs inlaid with birds and flowers.

Dutch marquetry chest of drawers of bombé shape, which belonged to Doris, Lady Vernon.

Queen Anne walnut tallboy.

PORCELAIN

The armorial porcelain is Chinese Export made c.1730 for Bowater Vernon. Here is displayed almost all that remains of what was probably an enormous multi-purpose service otherwise long smashed and discarded.

THE GOVERNESS'S ROOMS

In 1720/1 one of these rooms was 'the White Chamber hanged with Tapestry hangings'. The bed and its matching window curtains were made of camlet, a material originally made of a mixture of camel hair with either wool or silk – though by this date more likely goat's hair. It must have been extremely colourful, for it was striped in red and yellow and trimmed with yellow 'lace' (ie braid).

The present panelling may have been installed after the removal of the tapestries and has again been painted a stony white. The grey marble bolection chimney-piece is probably the original of about 1700. The room appears to be that listed as the governess's bedroom in the 1840 inventory.

PICTURES

Manner of FRANCIS WHEATLEY (1747–1801)
Portrait of a young girl

After Sir JOSHUA REYNOLDS, PRA (1723–92)
Lady Caroline Howard (1771–1848)
The daughter of the 5th Earl of Carlisle. The original is in the National Gallery, Washington.

J. McNEVIN
Lithographs of the exterior of Hanbury (showing the porch unglazed), the interior of the Hall, and the other Worcestershire house owned by the family at Shrawley Wood, all of the 1840s.

GEORGE VERTUE (1684–1756) after Sir GODFREY KNELLER (1646/9–1723)
Thomas Vernon (1654–1721)
The builder of Hanbury.

GEORGE PYNE (1801–84)
Watercolour of Sir Harry Vernon's room while an undergraduate at Christ Church, Oxford, c.1852.

Sir JAMES THORNHILL (1675–1734)
'Hanbury Hall from ye Bowling Green', c.1710
Photograph of the original drawing in the British Museum; see p.31.

J. ROSS
Engraving of Thomas Vernon's tomb in Hanbury church.

FURNITURE

Upright Broadwood piano, c.1840, given by Mrs Udale and her daughter.

Late Victorian doll's-house, given by the late Mrs Christopher Cadbury.

French boat bed, of the type mentioned in the 1840 inventory.

The Painted Staircase and Hall

THE GOTHICK CORRIDORS

In 1991 a riotous Gothick-patterned wallpaper of the 1830s was discovered here under later layers. It has been carefully copied, and the seven colours used may have originally been intended to complement the rich Baroque tones of Thornhill's murals. At the same time, small fragments of an earlier Gothick paper were found, and these are thought to date from the late 1770s, when Emma Vernon and her husband Henry Cecil were bringing the house up to date.

Two enriched doorcases in the eastern section of the corridor have pierced urns (perhaps intended to represent perfume burners) set in broken segmental pediments. The one seen straight ahead down the corridor from the Governess's Room is still *in situ,* and marked the entrance to Mrs Vernon's apartment, which consisted of four rooms: a little dressing-room, followed by 'My Lady's Chamber', with another dressing-room and closet beyond in the north-east pavilion. The other doorcase has been re-sited, but probably stood on the landing at the head of the White Staircase (see plan on p.6), giving access to two further bedchambers – listed in 1720/1 as the 'Chamber over the lobby' and the 'Chamber over the Great Parlour'. The corridor leading to them was then hung with ten maps.

PICTURES

After Sir JOSHUA REYNOLDS, PRA (1723–92)
Master Williams-Wynn as the infant St John

ENGLISH, *c.*1780
Thomas Shrawley Vernon (1759–1825)
Oval
His son, Thomas Tayler Vernon, inherited Hanbury in 1829.

ENGLISH, *c.*1830
? Jessie Foley, Mrs Thomas Tayler Vernon
Oval

FURNITURE

Late Georgian oak settee and chairs in the Gothick taste.

The model of a large country house made of shells, mica and various other materials is an example of Victorian 'lady's work'. Some of the elements, including the figures, may have been from a kit.

IN LOBBY OUTSIDE CEDAR BEDROOM:

Gilt-gesso mirror, early eighteenth-century.
Long-case clock. Mahogany and satinwood case, nineteenth-century.

CERAMICS

Most of the porcelain in the black cabinet belonged to Doris, Lady Vernon (see separate handlist).

THE CEDAR BEDROOM

This room, described as the 'Chamber over the Great Parlour' in 1720/1, was originally the largest bedroom in the house, incorporating what is now the lobby outside, and part of the adjoining bathroom. It seems to have been cut down to its present size in 1860, to judge by a sketch of that date, signed by an architect named D. Webster. A scheme of simple brown paintwork was discovered under later layers on the panelling, and may be of the same date. It has been carefully copied by the National Trust.

FURNITURE

Apart from the half-tester bed of about 1840 (from Sherborne Park, Gloucestershire), the furnishings of the room all originated from Hanbury, but were bought by the National Trust at the auction of the contents of Shrawley Wood House in 1991.

TEXTILES

The rare Axminster carpet is late Georgian and was probably made for the antiquary Sir Samuel Rush Meyrick (1783–1848) of Goodrich Court, Herefordshire.

THE HERCULES BEDROOM

In 1720/1 this was the 'Chamber over the kitchen', with a dressing-room and closet beyond in the north-west 'pavilion'. The room takes its present name from the figure of Hercules surmounting the corner chimney-piece in the Dressing Room. The closet (not shown to visitors) is now a bathroom, but originally contained 'two Dutch Chairs with blew Cushions thereon', a table and a walnut close stool.

In the bedchamber itself, the panelling (or wainscot) was 'painted with Flakestone', possibly a type of grey and white marbling. The bed here was of 'Sky Colour damask lined with white Sattin Embroidered', and the furniture included a lacquer cabinet on a gilt stand, and an inlaid table between the windows with candlestands on either side and a 'great glass' above it. The richness of these furnishings suggests that it was one of the most important bedchambers in the house, enjoying splendid views over Thomas Vernon's formal parterre, recently replanted by the National Trust.

CHIMNEY-PIECE

The room still has its original bolection-moulded marble chimney-piece with a diamond-shaped panel – an unusual device – giving emphasis to the chimney-breast.

TAPESTRY

Flemish, late seventeenth-century.

PICTURES

The flower paintings are from the Watney collection.

Two engravings of hunting scenes by Bernard Baron after Wootton (V) hang in the passage outside, and give a good idea of life at Hanbury in Bowater Vernon's day.

Three unused designs for the front of Hanbury Hall are in the passage, just outside the Hercules Bedroom doorway.

FURNITURE

The satinwood bed is from Lodge Park, Sherborne.

Satinwood toilet table, c.1790, with its original fittings.

The French provincial wardrobe has particularly fine keyplates.

CERAMICS

The glazed cabinet in the passage outside belonged to Doris, Lady Vernon and contains porcelain, mostly from the Worcester factory, from her collection.

THE HERCULES DRESSING ROOM

CHIMNEY-PIECE

This room contains a charmingly detailed corner chimney-piece, flanked by Doric pilasters, and with its original overmantel like a section of an ogee dome. Such chimney-pieces became popular in England in the reign of William and Mary, particularly for dressing-rooms and closets, where three fireplaces could share the same flue, and where extra warmth was provided by bringing them further into the room. Examples with tiered shelves for the display of porcelain can be found at Wren's Hampton Court, at Beningbrough Hall near York,

The Hercules Dressing Room in the 1950s

and in the contemporary engravings of Daniel Marot, who referred to corner chimney-pieces of this kind as 'cheminées à l'angloise'.

SCULPTURE

The statuette of Hercules, given by the late Mr Robert Vernon Harcourt, is a modern version of the original, stolen in the 1960s.

FURNITURE

The Queen Anne bureau and the red japanned chairs are recent bequests to the National Trust. The chairs are attributable to the London cabinetmaker Giles Grendey (1693–1780), who made a huge suite of similar furniture for the Spanish market in the late 1730s. They are appropriately placed here, as in 1720/1 the room contained 'a red Japan looking glass' and 'boxes of the same'.

TEXTILES

The two needlework pictures are mid-eighteenth-century, with contemporary frames and glazing.

The back staircase outside the Hercules Dressing Room was built in 1988 within the shell of a Victorian extension and takes its cue from another secondary staircase in the house. It descends to the shop and tea-rooms, which occupy part of the original kitchen quarters.

PICTURE

Election poster, painted on canvas, from Thomas Vernon's time as Whig MP for Worcester (1715–21). On the left is Worcester Cathedral with the legend 'For Peace and the Church of England by Law Established', and on the right are ships at sea, 'For Trade and the Good of our Country'. In the centre is a portrait of George I.

THE LONG GALLERY

As can be seen on the 1732 perspective view of Hanbury, the Long Gallery was always detached from the house – an unusual arrangement, suggesting that it might have formed part of an earlier Elizabethan or Jacobean house on the site. However, the brickwork appears to be of the same date as the house, except for the curiously shaped Victorian loggia at the southern end. The building could have been inspired by the famous Water Gallery at Hampton Court, demolished by William III after Queen Mary's death in 1694.

Inside, the main room is panelled to shoulder height. Of the two Jacobean overmantels, the first is made up of woodwork from a church and is carved with the symbols of the Passion. It frames a painted canvas of the Vernon arms ('or, a fesse azure with three sheaves or thereon and a crosslet fitchy gules in chief'). The marble bolection chimney-piece below it is original, of about 1700. The second Jacobean overmantel, which may have been made from a bed-head, has recently been set up at the end of the Long Gallery after being moved from the Smoking Room, or Oak Room, as it was previously known. It is elaborately carved in oak, the three compartments divided by caryatids and crowned by a frieze with fruit, flowers and strapwork. In the centre are the Prince of Wales's feathers and below the figures are the thistle, rose, fleur-de-lis and the pear of Worcestershire with Stuart crowns. It is said by the family to have come from Tickenhill House, Bewdley, which was intended by James I to be a residence for his eldest son, Prince Henry, the first Prince of Wales entitled to use the thistle. Tickenhill House was being dismantled at the time Hanbury was being built and a relation of Thomas Vernon, William Vernon Caldwell, who was living nearby, is supposed to have helped acquire this overmantel.

In the 1720/1 inventory the Gallery contained a bureau or 'Scriptore with looking glass doors', two globes on square tables, two large oval tables, a couch and a number of chairs, five of them covered in turkey-work. The walls were hung with maps. By 1790, however, the room had become a picture gallery, probably reflecting the taste of Bowater Vernon (d.1735) and his son and heir, Thomas (d.1771). A set of four 'fine Fish Pieces, by Ryback'

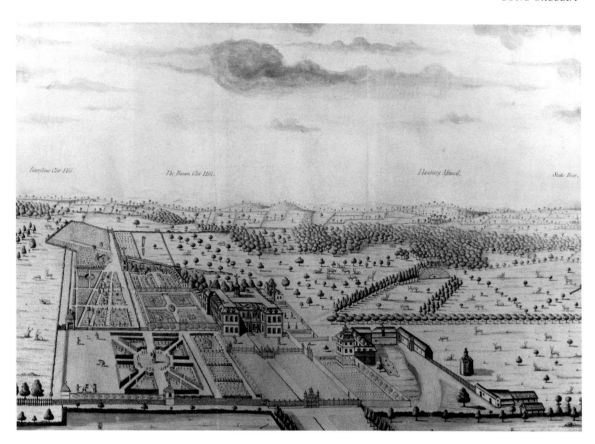

*Bird's-eye view of Hanbury Hall in 1732 by Joseph
Dougharty. The Long Gallery is the detached building
beyond the house. This unusual arrangement suggests that
the Long Gallery may have once formed part of an earlier
Elizabethan or Jacobean house on the site*

can probably be associated with three payments
made by Bowater to the painter Pieter Andreas
Rysbrack in 1734, and there were a number of other
still-lifes including a 'large capital Piece of Dead
Game, by *Barloe*' (ie Thomas Barlow).

The northernmost bay of the Long Gallery was
originally divided off as a closet, and beyond it, on
the east, was Thomas Vernon's study. It is a small
room wainscoted from floor to ceiling with
Jacobean panelling, probably from the old house at
Hanbury, and some of its original early eighteenth-
century shelves on pierced brackets. The 1720/1
inventory includes two writing desks and a long list

of books in the study adjoining the Gallery, so on
rainy days Thomas Vernon was able to combine
exercise in his Long Gallery with reading. Most of
these books were on legal, political and religious
subjects, but there were also some horticultural
treatises like 'The Compleat Gardiner by Monsieur
de la Quintine' (the superviser of Louis XIV's
orangery and kitchen gardens at Versailles). Vernon
also stored his legal papers and deeds in this room, all
kept in boxes meticulously listed in the inventory.

Below the Long Gallery is a simple tiled dairy and
cheese room which will be restored and shown in
due course.

CHAPTER TWO
THE GARDEN AND PARK

Around 1700 Thomas Vernon engaged George London (d.1714) to layout a formal garden on the south side of the house with walled enclosures, paired gazebos, parterres divided by straight paths, and compartments of box and yew in the Dutch style which prevailed during the reign of William and Mary. With his partner Henry Wise, London was the leading garden designer of the period, and from their nurseries at Brompton, Wise supervised the Royal gardens, including Hampton Court and Kensington, while London travelled all over the country and 'saw and gave Directions once or twice a year in most of the Noblemens and Gentlemens Gardens in England', according to his pupil Stephen Switzer. Such gardens were almost all swept away in the late eighteenth century, as at Dyrham Park in Gloucestershire, created by Thomas Vernon's contemporary William Blathwayt, and celebrated for its waterworks. But a modest example survives at Westbury Court (restored by the National Trust).

London was responsible for Dyrham and for Hampton Court, Herefordshire, among other gardens recorded in Kip's engravings, and at Hanbury two plans survive endorsed, perhaps in Vernon's hand, 'Mr. London's Draughts'. The first is for the wilderness (with its diagonal paths converging on the main walk) and the formal grove adjoining the bowling green. Both these features can be seen in the complete perspective drawing made in 1732 by the Worcester surveyor Joseph Dougharty, and attached to his estate survey of Hanbury. Wootton's portrait of Bowater Vernon in the Smoking Room contains another view of the formal garden, only two years later.

Both these views show a long central walk stretching out past the pond beyond the Long Gallery. This walk, and the pond itself, are among the only features of the formal layout to survive at Hanbury. (Beyond this is a mid-eighteenth-century

ice-house.) Dougharty shows gentlemen playing bowls in the south-east corner of the garden, and while Thornhill was painting the staircase about 1710, he also made a drawing entitled 'Hanbury Hall from ye Bowling Green'. This shows the young hedges still looking ragged, in contrast to their neat maturity drawn by Dougharty more than twenty years later.

Many of the other features seen in the bird's-eye view are confirmed by the bills of the painter Thomas Boulter, dating from 1718. These refer to the iron 'palasades' and the three pairs of gates in the forecourt; the 'Garden door at my lady's Closet' (see p.16); the upper and lower summer-houses (which he also calls pavilions), built at either end of a second straight walk, dividing the Wilderness from the main parterre; and the two little pedimented 'green houses' in the fruit garden outside the Long Gallery, flanking a *clairvoyée* which offered a view over the pond. Interestingly, he also painted the 'Bowl Box and Board' (ie the scoring board for the bowls players), which was kept in the 'lower pavilion'. Other bills mention a statue of Ceres and two other 'figures', the 'Sun Dyal', the 'Seat below the Wilderness', the 'fine Apples' (evidently finials on a pair of gate-piers), and a 'marble skreen' which appears to have had 'Two Collumns round' as well as a pediment.

One of the garden buildings evidently contained a mural by Thornhill showing Diana resting under a canopy attended by a cupid, since the artist's sketch in the British Museum is inscribed 'Picture in ye Garden at Hanbury'.

(Right) 'Hanbury Hall from ye Bowling Green'; by James Thornhill, c.1710

(Right, below) Hanbury Hall, from Dr Treadway Nash's 'History of Worcestershire', 1781

Archaeological investigation in the winter of 1992–3 uncovered many of the remains of this formal garden, including the foundations of one of the two 'green houses'. With the aid of a generous bequest from Dinah Albright and a grant from the European Union, the main outlines of the garden have now been reinstated. The 'Sunken Parterre' came first. Increasingly, this is being planted with greater historical accuracy, avoiding modern 'clumping' of plants, while the beds adjoining the raised terrace on three sides of the parterre have been planted with contrasting specimens on a regular tight grid, as laid down in early eighteenth-century publications. Originally, tall brick walls surrounded the parterre garden, but the reconstruction has substituted a yew hedge on cost grounds but also to avoid a mass of new brickwork to challenge the mature and subtle rose-red bricks of the Hall.

Also to avoid masonry detailing which might 'upstage' that of the Hall, the two pairs of garden pavilions so far reconstructed are made of timber:

the 'greenhouses' in the Fruit Garden next to the Gallery are versions in trellis (as often seen in engravings of early Dutch gardens) while the Bowling Green pavilions have wooden walls imitating rusticated stonework. The mid-1990s saw the Fountain Pool installed.

The 'Grove' was reinstated to George London's layout in 1999. The obelisk in the Wilderness, shown by Dougharty, but for which no historical detail is known, was re-created in timber in 2000, following a design, triangular on plan, by Batty Langley. The tall gate-piers either side of the Parterre Garden were reinstated in 2001, and the Bowling Green was reinstated on its original site in 2002.

The sweeping away of the formal gardens was probably begun by Thomas Vernon, after he came of age, in 1745 and continued by Emma and her husband Henry Cecil after 1771. Dr Treadway Nash's engraving of Hanbury, published in 1781, shows the forecourt and 'large stables and offices in full view' but there are no signs of any garden buildings.

The Parterre and Wilderness

A detail of the Sunken Parterre

THE FORECOURT

The original Forecourt gates were apparently sold to the owners of nearby Mere Hall in 1790, when the contents of the house were also dispersed, and the park must then have come right up to the entrance front. J. C. Buckler's watercolour of the house in 1833 shows deer grazing close up to the façade. It was not until 1856 that Thomas Bowater Vernon commissioned R. W. Billings to design a new forecourt with elaborate brick piers, archways and railings, and a pair of highly eccentric pavilions at the outer corners. Perhaps initially inspired by those seen on Dougharty's bird's-eye view, these are at the same time unmistakably Victorian with their scalloped tiles, wooden ceilings in Moorish taste, and brightly coloured Minton tiles. Billings's introduction to Thomas Vernon must have come

through his patron, the 10th Earl of Haddington, one of whose daughters was married to the Rector of Hanbury, while another was to marry Thomas's brother and heir, Sir Harry, in 1861. The Forecourt walls have lost their elaborate iron railings, seen between the piers in early photographs, but have now been wired up for climbers, which smother them with foliage and flowers in summer.

THE ORANGERY

The handsome mid-eighteenth-century Orangery may be discovered by following one of the paths leading westwards past the Wilderness, and emerging on an open lawn flanked by ilexes. It does not appear on Dougharty's view of 1732, or the Wootton painting of 1734, and probably dates from

The Orangery

after 1745, when Thomas Vernon, the builder's grandson, came of age. Among the papers of his father, Bowater Vernon, is a 'Method of raising orange trees from Genoa', but his plants were probably kept in the two 'green houses' in the fruit garden, next to the Long Gallery. As originally built, the Orangery would have been at the western extremity of the garden shown by Dougharty, and would have looked over a low wall or ha-ha straight into the park. It was only later, after 1771, that Emma Vernon and her husband Henry Cecil greatly extended the garden in this direction by building the present ha-ha further south.

The building can be compared with other orangeries seen in the watercolours of the Rococo artist Thomas Robins, made in the 1740s and '50s. It is built of finely coursed red brick, with a basket of fruit and flowers carved in stone in the pediment. Three large stone vases surmount the central section, and on the corners are two pineapple finials, possibly the pair described in Thomas Boulter's bill of 1718, when they surmounted a pair of gate-piers. Oranges and lemons are again being grown here, and in the summer are placed outside in their Versailles tubs.

The mushroom-house behind the Orangery (to the right) is a lean-to addition of the 1860s. It can now be seen producing mushrooms for the Hall once again.

THE PARK

On the north and east sides of the garden, Dougharty's view of 1732 depicts the deer-park with its avenues; the 'Exact Plan of Hanbury Hall Gardens and Park' in the survey calls these 'The Lime Tree Walk in Length, 584 yards' and 'The Long Walk in Length 633 yards'. Near the latter is the curious feature called 'The Semicircle', recently partly reinstated. One of George London's surviving plans is for this amphitheatre, 365 feet wide, planted with trees in the different quarters and intended as a kind of viewing platform, for it is annotated like a topographical view with vistas to the Malverns, Berrow Hill, Woodberry Hill, Abberley, the Brown Clee, Titterstone Clee, Kinver Edge, the Clents, the Lickeys and several church steeples. Most of these can still be seen.

(Right) A view of one of the garden pavilions

CHAPTER THREE

THE ARCHITECTURE OF
THE HOUSE

The post-Restoration country house associated with the age of Wren owes little to Sir Christopher and much to Sir Roger Pratt and Hugh May. Its architecture is astylar (ie without columns or pilasters) and usually consists of two storeys, broad eaves, hipped roofs with dormer windows and sometimes a cupola. This 'infinitely endearing pattern' originated with Clarendon House, Piccadilly, in the 1660s, and examples are Ramsbury, Belton, Uppark and Denham, all dating from the 1680s. It was repeated by the gentry and their provincial architect-craftsmen with great felicity all over England. Hanbury is a late example of brick with stone dressings, if the date 1701 carved in Victorian numerals above the front door is to be believed, and has some relatively old-fashioned features, suggesting that it was designed by a conservative master mason rather than a London architect in the vanguard of fashion.

Firstly, the wings are returned to project also on the side elevations, forming independent pavilions at the corners 'in the French pavilion way', as John Evelyn wrote of Montagu House, designed by Robert Hooke in the 1670s and built on the future

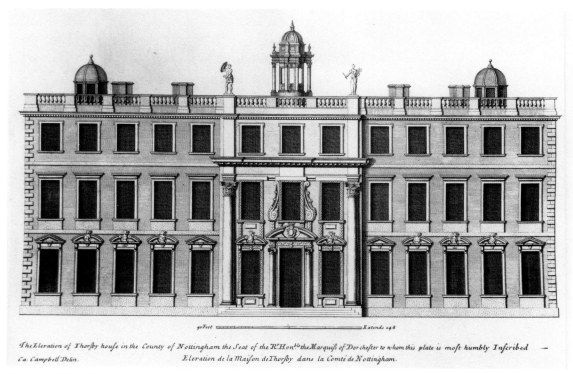

Thoresby Hall, Nottinghamshire, from Colen Campbell's 'Vitruvius Britannicus', 1715

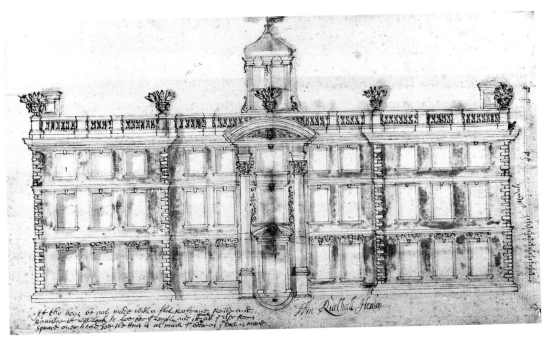

Design for the entrance front of Hanbury by William Rudhall

Design for the entrance front by Jon Chatterton

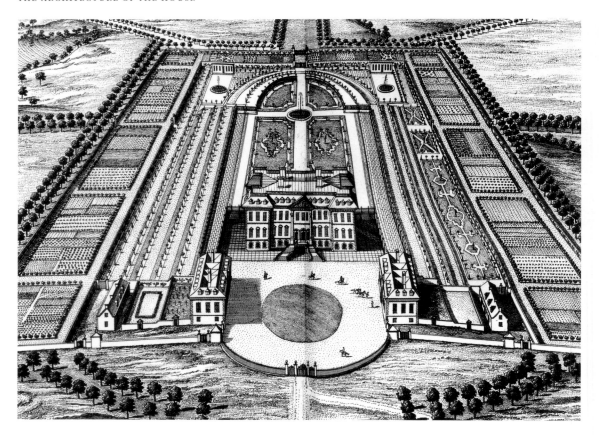

Bird's-eye view of Ragley Hall, Warwickshire, engraved by Kip

site of the British Museum. Hooke was also the architect of Ragley (1679–83), only eight miles away in Warwickshire. However, the corner pavilions at Hanbury may have been an afterthought. Recent investigation has revealed signs of a pair of window openings in the timbering which separates the Dining Room from the north-east pavilion. Presumably it was during the construction of the east front that Thomas Vernon decided on a much grander house with pavilions.

Secondly, the architect of Hanbury copied his centrepiece almost exactly from William Talman's vanished Nottinghamshire house, Thoresby, which had a giant Corinthian order of half-columns spaced astride three bays and a centre window enriched with carved fruit and scrolls, according to the engraving in volume I of Colen Campbell's *Vitruvius Britannicus* (1715). Thoresby was Talman's first house, built in 1683 and again after a fire in 1685–7. Here, for the first time, he replaced the traditional hipped roof with an attic storey and balustrade in a continuous façade, giving a monumental effect, derived from engravings of Roman and Genoese palaces.

Three drawings for the entrance front of Hanbury, all by different hands, have survived (see pp.36–7). Each shows a front of eleven bays with projecting wings of three bays. The most detailed is signed by William Rudhall (*c*.1660–1733) of Henley-in-Arden, Warwickshire. He displays precise

(Opposite) The entrance front, which is dated (in Victorian numerals) 1701

The clock on the north face of the cupola

knowledge of Talman's Thoresby with the monumental attic storey and balustrade hiding the diminished mansard roof and with the giant Corinthian order and the enriched centrepiece, here clumsily confined to one central bay. If the open cupola at Thoresby was built as shown by Colen Campbell, it was not reinstated after the fire; but one was certainly built at Hanbury. Rudhall's drawing is inscribed: 'if the house be not made with a flat Roof and Rail and Banister it will look to Loe for ye Length and itt [will] make all ye new Rooms Square overhead soe the Hous is as much ye better as ye cost is more'. Vernon ignored all this advice and the 'long and low' criticism might still perhaps be levelled at the garden front.

Ragley originally had a balustrade above the hipped roof, as proposed by 'Mr. Withenbury's Draught for a Best ffront' at Hanbury. All we know of James Withenbury is that he was the Worcester mason responsible for the monument to Bishop Lloyd (d.1718) in Fladbury church, Worcestershire.

About the author of the third drawing inscribed 'Draught of building Jon Chatterton's of a Best front' we know even less.

William Rudhall's name crops up again at Hanbury, in a note scribbled on sheets accompanying the painter, Mr Boulter's bill of 1718: 'Paid Mr. Rudhall for the chimneypiece of the Pink Chamber £1.5.0'. So he probably remains the likeliest candidate as architect. But whether he worked at Ragley earlier in his career, or whether he had first-hand knowledge of Talman's Thoresby remains a mystery. According to Kip's view of Ragley, the essence of the Thoresby centrepiece, that is the two widely spaced giant columns with separate entablatures, a feature of Dutch origin, was already envisaged by Robert Hooke in 1679–83, and, moreover, beneath a pediment. Ragley is the direct model of Hanbury in several ways and thus Thomas Vernon, by looking to his neighbour, obtained the old-fashioned-looking house he desired.

Recent research has given us a clearer picture of how Hanbury was gradually expanded; Vernon seems to have changed his mind repeatedly. He began with the north front, which faced a service court and was the only unbalanced elevation, perhaps incorporating the remains of an earlier house on the site. Its late seventeenth-century centre, which houses the Smoking Room of the present house, has diapered brickwork and rather narrower windows than are found elsewhere – still described as having 'transome window frames' in 1809. From here the house grew clockwise in ranges one room deep. The east front (containing the present Dining Room and Drawing Room) may well have been intended as a perfectly conventional Midlands Smith of Warwick-style, seven-bay front with a central doorway. But fairly early on in the work a south-east pavilion was added. The Great Hall and staircase range must have followed. The long west front with more corner pavilions completed the building.

CHAPTER FOUR
THE VERNONS OF HANBURY

The ancient Vernon lineage stems from Richard, Lord of Vernon in Normandy, who was made an English baron in the reign of William the Conqueror. The Vernons of Haddon in Derbyshire, and those commemorated by the beautiful tombs at Tong in Shropshire, are the forebears of the senior branch of the family, represented today by Lord Vernon, of Poynton in Cheshire and Sudbury in Derbyshire. Sudbury Hall, built and decorated by George Vernon over a long period from 1665 to the 1690s, belongs to the generation before Hanbury and came to the Trust in 1965. A cadet branch settled in early Plantagenet times at Wheatcroft, near Northwich, in Cheshire, and it is from this branch of the family that the Vernons of Hanbury are descended.

The Rev. Richard Vernon became Rector of Hanbury in 1580 and held the post for the next 47 years. He married Frances, daughter of John Wylde of Astwood, a substantial farmhouse in half-timber and brick still standing in the parish and portrayed on the title-page of the Hanbury estate survey of 1731. He died in 1627 leaving numerous offspring, as his monument in the church testifies. His eldest son Edward purchased in 1631 from the Leighton family the manor and advowson of Hanbury, in the rectory of which he had been born and brought up. Edward Vernon suffered at the hands of both sides in the Civil War. He was succeeded by his son Richard in 1666, whose son, Thomas Vernon, the rebuilder of Hanbury, succeeded in 1679.

Thomas Vernon was born at Hanbury in 1655 and became an eminent Chancery barrister. He was called to the Bar in 1679, was a bencher of the Middle Temple in 1703 and practised in the Court of Chancery for 40 years, by which means he amassed a large fortune and greatly increased his family property in Worcestershire. In 1715 he was elected to the House of Commons for the City of Worcester, as a Whig, and held the seat until his death in 1721. He is buried at Hanbury and his excellent monument, by the sculptors Edward Stanton and Christopher Horsnaile, is in the parish church.

A somewhat eulogistic character sketch of Vernon appeared in 1706 in a poem entitled *Corona Civica*, addressed to 'The Right Honorable the Lord-Keeper of the Great Seal':

Experienc'd *Vernon* joy'd your Worth's *Success*,
Polite his *Manner*, winning his *Address*,
Strong to confute and easie to express,
Causes unnumber'd no *Fatigue* create
To his vers'd mind, nor has the Burden Weight.
A Look serene his clear *Discernment* shows,
Law has no puzzling *Doubt* to knit his *Brows*;
Secure of Fame he flies a loftier Fate,
Content with Riches in a safer State.

Vernon is best remembered for his *Reports of Cases decided in Chancery, 1681–1718*. These were private notes made to aid his memory but were published, after his death, by Lord Chancellor Macclesfield after a legal dispute between his widow and his heir, and were highly regarded in Chancery proceedings for many years. Despite his great name in Law and his staunch Whig principles, Vernon never held any public office, though at one moment the Lord Chancellorship was almost within his grasp. This was at the time of the first split in the Whig party. Lady Cowper in her diary (1716) states that it was proposed to put out her husband and make Vernon Lord Chancellor in his place. Nothing, however, came of this and Lord Cowper kept the Seal.

In 1679 Thomas Vernon married Mary Keck, daughter of Sir Anthony Keck, who was, like his son-in-law, a successful barrister. There were, however, no children and after Mary's death in 1733, Hanbury went to a cousin, Bowater Vernon,

whom the county historian Dr Treadway Nash describes as 'a man of weak mind . . . his head was giddy and he launched in every species of Vanity and Extravagance', squandering his benefactor's fortune. He died in 1735 and his monument, sometimes ascribed to Roubiliac but more likely by Sir Henry Cheere, is in Hanbury church. Happily, his son Thomas, Nash's special friend, was 'a man of great parts', prudence and virtue, restoring the Hanbury estates and representing the City of Worcester in Parliament from 1746 to 1761. He died prematurely in 1771 leaving a widow, Emma Cornewall from Berrington in Herefordshire, and an only daughter Emma, still a girl in her teens.

Mrs Vernon at once set about finding a grand husband for her heiress daughter and a match was made with Henry Cecil, nephew and heir to the 9th Earl of Exeter. But the marriage in 1776, as predicted by Dr Treadway Nash, who was for a time Emma's guardian, was most unfortunate. In spite of Emma's £6,000 and his £3,000 a year, 'they ran themselves aground and were obliged to break up housekeeping, but what was worse, they both entreagued'. At the time he married, Cecil seems to have been a selfish, extravagant young man, though later, when he succeeded as Lord Exeter, he became a sober and almost praiseworthy character. According to the indignant Dr Nash, he drove his 'late, unfortunate friend's daughter . . . to Norris's drops and Madeira'. So it was hardly surprising that this passionate, headstrong girl should have fallen in love with the Hanbury curate, William Sneyd, a well-educated but somewhat weak young man, who was likewise a consumptive. They eloped together in 1789.

This was a sobering shock for Henry Cecil. Rather than face the sneers of his neighbours and the demands of his creditors, he absconded from Hanbury and appeared later at the village of Great Bolas in Shropshire, where he called himself John Jones and took lodgings with a farmer called Hoggins.

(Left) Monument to Thomas Vernon (1654–1721); by Edward Stanton and Christopher Horsnaile (Hanbury church)

(Right) Monument to Bowater Vernon (1683–1735); probably by Sir Henry Cheere (Hanbury church)

The farmer had a daughter named Sally, a pretty sweet-natured girl, and soon enough Cecil had compromised her. Farmer Hoggins, finding out, forced Cecil, more or less at gunpoint, to go through a marriage ceremony with his daughter. 'John Jones', as an unwilling bigamist, was in a horrible position. Secretly he set in motion divorce proceedings against Emma, and a decree was granted by the House of Lords in 1791. Immediately he took Sally to London and married her again. In her country simplicity she accepted his trumped-up explanation and they returned to live quietly in Great Bolas. Telling Sally nothing, he took her across England to the Cecil family seat, Burghley near Stamford in Lincolnshire. Arriving after dark, Sally was astonished to be received with great respect by the servants and addressed as 'my Lady'. She almost collapsed at the shock and could never get used to her great position. The story of Henry Cecil and his 'Cottage Countess' is told, but very inaccurately, by Tennyson in his poem 'The Lord of Burleigh', and most sympathetically by Elizabeth Inglis-Jones in her book on the subject.

Emma, meanwhile, had married Will Sneyd in 1791. However, his consumption got worse and she took him to Lisbon, where the air was then thought to be good for that complaint. There he died on 2 August 1793. She returned to England where in 1795 she married, for the third time, John Phillips, a native of Droitwich, who was her late husband's friend and executor. To be near their Worcestershire friends, they settled at a house called Winterdyne near the river at Bewdley, but in 1804, on the death of Henry Cecil (by now 10th Earl and 1st Marquess of Exeter), Emma returned to Hanbury and her restored inheritance. With her third husband she lived quietly and charitably at Hanbury until her death in 1818. According to her directions she was buried not in the Vernon vault in the church but in a simple grave which may still be seen against the north boundary of the churchyard. She was wrapped by her faithful maid in the sheet that had covered Will Sneyd's body at his death.

John Phillips continued to live at Hanbury until 1829, but gave up his life interest in that year in favour of Emma's distant cousin and heir, Thomas Shrawley Vernon, grandson of Bowater Vernon's brother. For the ensuing century staider times were to prevail at Hanbury. Thomas Tayler Vernon has a monument in the church by Chantrey (1837) and his eldest son, Thomas Bowater Vernon, made extensive alterations to the house in 1856–9. The latter never married and so was succeeded by his younger brother, Sir Harry Foley Vernon, created baronet in 1885, who devoted his long life to county work and his Worcestershire estates. He married Lady Georgina Baillie-Hamilton, daughter of the 10th Earl of Haddington, and died in 1920 at the age of 86. By the terms of the will of his son, Sir George Vernon, 2nd Baronet, who died in 1940, Hanbury came to the National Trust in 1953 by means of an endowment provided by an anonymous donor.

James Lees-Milne has written of his visits to Sir George in 1938, on behalf of the Trust, and then after his death to his long estranged widow, Doris: 'I fancy she was one of those people who invited, if they did not positively relish, disaster. She could not open a bazaar without twisting her ankle on the way to the platform. She could not go shopping in Droitwich without having her handbag rifled.' Lady Vernon lived in two rooms 'in apparent dingy penury' until the house was restored in 1953. She continued at Hanbury until she died in 1962.

(Left) Emma Vernon (1755–1818); by Sir Joshua Reynolds (Dining Room)

(Right) Henry Cecil, 10th Earl of Exeter, and his second wife, Sally ('the Cottage Countess'); by Sir Thomas Lawrence (Burghley House, Cambridgeshire)

FAMILY TREE OF THE VERNONS

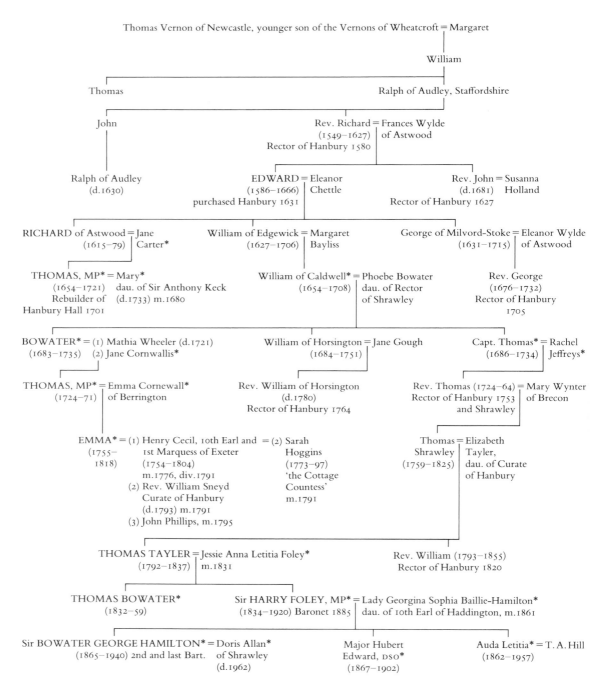

Thomas Vernon of Newcastle, younger son of the Vernons of Wheatcroft = Margaret
|
William
|
Thomas   Ralph of Audley, Staffordshire
|
John   Rev. Richard = Frances Wylde
     (1549–1627) of Astwood
     Rector of Hanbury 1580

Ralph of Audley   EDWARD = Eleanor   Rev. John = Susanna
(d.1630)   (1586–1666) Chettle   (d.1681) Holland
     purchased Hanbury 1631   Rector of Hanbury 1627

RICHARD of Astwood = Jane   William of Edgewick = Margaret   George of Milvord-Stoke = Eleanor Wylde
(1615–79) Carter*   (1627–1706) Bayliss   (1631–1715) of Astwood

THOMAS, MP* = Mary*   William of Caldwell* = Phoebe Bowater   Rev. George
(1654–1721) dau. of Sir Anthony Keck   (1654–1708) dau. of Rector   (1676–1732)
Rebuilder of (d.1733) m.1680   of Shrawley   Rector of Hanbury
Hanbury Hall 1701   1705

BOWATER* = (1) Mathia Wheeler (d.1721)   William of Horsington = Jane Gough   Capt. Thomas* = Rachel
(1683–1735) (2) Jane Cornwallis*   (1684–1751)   (1686–1734) Jeffreys*

THOMAS, MP* = Emma Cornewall*   Rev. William of Horsington   Rev. Thomas (1724–64) = Mary Wynter
(1724–71) of Berrington   (d.1780)   Rector of Hanbury 1753 of Brecon
         Rector of Hanbury 1764   and Shrawley

EMMA* = (1) Henry Cecil, 10th Earl and = (2) Sarah   Thomas = Elizabeth
(1755–   1st Marquess of Exeter   Hoggins   Shrawley Tayler,
1818)   (1754–1804)   (1773–97)   (1759–1825) dau. of Curate
       m.1776, div.1791   'the Cottage   of Hanbury
    (2) Rev. William Sneyd   Countess'
       Curate of Hanbury   m.1791
       (d.1793) m.1791
    (3) John Phillips, m.1795

THOMAS TAYLER = Jessie Anna Letitia Foley*   Rev. William (1793–1855)
(1792–1837) m.1831   Rector of Hanbury 1820

THOMAS BOWATER*   Sir HARRY FOLEY, MP* = Lady Georgina Sophia Baillie-Hamilton*
(1832–59)   (1834–1920) Baronet 1885 dau. of 10th Earl of Haddington, m.1861

Sir BOWATER GEORGE HAMILTON* = Doris Allan*   Major Hubert   Auda Letitia* = T. A. Hill
(1865–1940) 2nd and last Bart. of Shrawley   Edward, DSO*   (1862–1957)
                  (d.1962)   (1867–1902)

Owners of the house are in capitals   *indicates a portrait in the house (including photographs)

CHAPTER FIVE
THE RESTORATION OF HANBURY

Following Lady Vernon's death in 1962, the National Trust undertook further basic repairs and the sort of rationalisation regretted by a later generation, including the demolition, without record, of the service wing linking the main house with the Long Gallery. Because the major interest at Hanbury, apart from the entrance front, was considered to be the Thornhill murals, only two rooms were made available for the public to see, and the house was let as a family home.

A second letting came to grief in 1977, when the Trust felt that it was no longer possible to find a private occupant who would give the degree of public access required by a burgeoning National Trust membership. Some key portraits returned from Shrawley Wood House; Robert Watney gave English porcelain figures, flower paintings and furniture; and redecoration and furnishings were funded by the Merrill Trust. But the house attracted few visitors compared with other historic houses in the area. By the late 1980s, when it again required major expenditure, Hanbury had become a serious drain on the Trust's general funds.

A solution was found when it was decided to channel to Hanbury the many requests for conference facilities which the Trust receives, and which its duty to conserve important contents makes it difficult to accommodate elsewhere. The house is relatively robust, its layout is particularly helpful, and original contents were few.

With this use in mind, the main rooms have been largely refurnished and partly redecorated. At the same time, it has been possible to work out the original plan of about 1700 through studying the inventories of 1720/1 and 1829, and the 1790 sale catalogue, as well as by examining the recently opened-up structure.

No sooner had the National Trust embarked on this work than Mr Horton, widower of Sir George's adopted daughter, died, and following her specific wish left the Trust what he knew had come from Hanbury: the rest of the family portraits, crested silver, Chinese Export porcelain made for Bowater Vernon in about 1730, and the splendid pier-glass with the Vernon arms, now in the Blue Bedroom. He believed that the remaining furniture at Shrawley Wood House had not come from Hanbury. However, as it was removed to the saleroom, suspicions were confirmed by many 1940s carrier's labels, previously hidden, endorsed 'Miss Vernon, Hanbury Hall'. At the ensuing sales Mr Wolf, the Droitwich antique dealer and old friend who had helped the Hortons build splendid oriental and other collections at Shrawley, was able to pronounce on what had or had not come from Hanbury Hall.

BIBLIOGRAPHY

The Vernon family papers are in the Worcestershire County Record Office in Worcester (catalogue: 1974, ref.7335; also ref.3803, 1962 and 8041, 1977).

ASLET, Clive, 'Thoresby Hall, Nottinghamshire', *Country Life*, clxv, 28 June 1979, pp.2082–5.

CROFT-MURRAY, Edward, *Decorative Painting in England, 1537–1837*, i, 1962.

DOWNES, Kerry, *English Baroque Architecture*, 1966.

GENT, Margaret, 'Hanbury Hall: An Account of the House 1700 to 1860', MA Dissertation, Birmingham Polytechnic, 1992 (unpublished).

HABINGTON, Thomas, *Survey of Worcestershire, 1717 and 1733*, Worcestershire Historical Society, i, pp.253–4.

HARRIS, John, 'Thoresby House, Nottinghamshire', *Architectural History*, iv, 1961; vi, 1963.

HAWORTH, Jeffrey, 'Hanbury Hall, Worcestershire', *Country Life*, 12 December 1991, pp.48–51.

HILL, Oliver, and CORNFORTH, John, *English Country Houses: Caroline*, 1966.

INGLIS-JONES, Elizabeth, *The Lord of Burghley*, 1964.

JACKSON-STOPS, Gervase, 'A Baroque House and its Use: Hanbury Hall and the Inventory of 1721', *Apollo*, May 1994.

KINGSLEY, Nicholas, 'Anthony Keck', *Country Life*, 20 and 27 October, 1988.

LEES-MILNE, James, 'Hanbury Hall', *Country Life*, cxliii, 4 January 1968, pp.18–22; 11 January 1968, pp.66–70.

LEES-MILNE, James, *English Country Houses: Baroque*, 1970, p.124.

LEES-MILNE, James, *People and Places: Country House Donors and the National Trust*, 1992, pp.43–52.

NASH, The Rev. Dr Treadway, *Collections for the History of Worcestershire*, 1781.

SMITH, Brian S., *The Dougharty Family of Worcester, Estate Surveyors and Mapmakers 1700–60*, Worcestershire Historical Society, new series, v, 1967.

VERNON, Thomas, *Reports of Cases decided in Chancery, 1681–1718*, 1726–8 (ed. Lord Macclesfield); 1806–7 (ed. Lord Eldon).